Introduction

Thank You For Downloading This Cook

    Pumpkin Pie

    Light Pumpkin Pie

    Sour Cream Pumpkin Pie

    Pumpkin Orange Pie

    Crustless Pumpkin Pie

    Pecan Pumpkin Pie

    Pumpkin Bourbon Pie

    Pumpkin Rum Pie

    Apple Pumpkin Pie

    Pumpkin Dutch Apple Pie

    Pumpkin Mousse Pie

    Double Layer Pumpkin Pie

    Chocolate Pumpkin Pie

    Spiced Pumpkin Pie

    Gingersnap Pumpkin Pie

    Pumpkin Chiffon Pie

    No-Bake Pumpkin Pie

    Pumpkin Ice Cream Pie

    Praline Pumpkin Pie

    Frozen Pumpkin Pie

    Cheese Pumpkin Swirl Pie

    Pumpkin Cream Cheese Pie

    Pumpkin Hazelnut Pie

    Almond Pumpkin Pie

    Apple Butter Pumpkin Pie

    Mini Pumpkin Pies

    Pumpkin Caramel-Crunch Pie

    Maple Pumpkin Pie

    Upside Down Pumpkin Pie Cake

    Tofu Pumpkin Pie

Ingredients

    Pumpkin Pie with Pecan Brittle Topping

Pumpkin Banana Meringue Pies

Ingredients

Pumpkin Meringue Pie

Coconut Pumpkin Pie

Custard Pumpkin Pie

Pumpkin Squash Pie

Ingredients

Sweet Potato Pumpkin Pie

Decadent Chocolate Pumpkin Pie

Banana Pumpkin Mousse Pie

Maple-Walnut Pumpkin Pie

Persimmon-Pumpkin Pie

Toffee Pumpkin Pie

Chocolate Cream Pumpkin Pie

Pumpkin Banana Mousse Pie

Vanilla Pumpkin Pie

Pumpkin Walnut Pie

Caramel-Pecan Pumpkin Pie

Spicy Pumpkin Pie

Honey Pumpkin Pie

Pumpkin Mincemeat Pie

Author Page

One Last Thing:

Introduction

Pumpkins are a great ingredient in many baked goods and treats. I know many people who can not wait for this time of the year to enjoy several different types of pumpkin recipes.

This cookbook offers a wide variety of recipes for Pumpkin Pie.

I truly hope you enjoy the book and find some great recipes to try out!

Pumpkin Pie

The traditional pumpkin pie that has been enjoyed by all, all year round.

Ingredients

- 1 egg, beaten
- 1 tablespoon of flour
- ¾ cup of sugar
- 1 teaspoon of salt
- 1 ½ cups of canned pumpkin
- 1 ½ cups of evaporated milk
- 1 teaspoon of cinnamon
- 1 teaspoon of ginger
- ½ teaspoon of nutmeg
- 2 tablespoons of corn syrup
- 1 pastry for a single crust pie, 9 inch

Directions

Preheat oven to 450F.

Into a bowl, whisk sugar incrementally with the canned pumpkin, until smooth. Gradually stir in the salt, flour, cinnamon, ginger and nutmeg. Mix in corn syrup, beat the mixture until well combined. Beat in egg, and then gradually stir in the evaporated milk, mixing until well incorporated. Spread the pumpkin pie batter into your unbaked pie shell.

Bake for about 10 min then reduce oven heat to 325F and continue baking for another 30 min or until a toothpick inserted comes out clean.

Light Pumpkin Pie

The traditional pumpkin pie minus 100 calories per slice.

Ingredients

- 1 cup of ginger snaps, crumbled
- 1 (16 oz.) can of pumpkin puree
- 1/2 cup of egg whites
- 1/2 cup of white sugar
- 2 teaspoons of pumpkin pie spice
- 1 (12 oz.) can of evaporated skim milk

Direction

Preheat oven to 350F. Lightly grease a 9-inch glass pie pan.

Press evenly cookie crumbs into the bottom of the pan.

Into a mixing bowl, mix the rest of the ingredients. Pour into the crust and bake for about 45 min or until toothpick inserted in the centre comes out clean Allow to cool and slice into 8 wedges. Store covered inside the fridge.

Serve each wedge with a fat free whipped cream

Sour Cream Pumpkin Pie

The flaky pie crust and the rich spicy pumpkin filling altogether raise the real value of this pie.

Ingredients

Pie dough

1½ cups of flour

3 tablespoons of sugar

1 teaspoon of salt

¾ cup of cold unsalted butter, cubed

2½ tablespoons of vegetable shortening, cubed

¼ cup ice water

Filling

1 cup of pumpkin puree, unsweetened

2 eggs

¼ cup of sugar

½ cup of brown sugar

2 tablespoons of butter, melted, cooled

¾ cup of heavy cream

⅓ cup of sour cream

2 teaspoons of cinnamon

2 teaspoons of ginger

¼ teaspoon of ground cloves

¼ teaspoon of nutmeg

¼ teaspoon of salt

4 tablespoons of rum

2 teaspoons of vanilla extract

Topping – whipped cream

Directions

For Pie Crust:

Preheat oven to 400F.

Into the bowl of a mixer fitted with metal paddles, combine flour, sugar and salt; pulse just to combine. Pulse to cut in the butter and shortening until crumbly. Gradually add water while pulsing until stiff dough is formed.

Form dough into a disk, wrap and chill for an hour. The dough can be stored in the fridge for up to 5 days or frozen for up to a month.

Press dough into a pie plate, wrap and chill again.

Grease the shiny side of a tin foil, tightly fit the foil, greased side down, against the crust and fill with baking weights. Put the pie plate on a baking sheet and bake for about 25 min. Remove weights and foil press down some puffed crusts. Return the crust to the oven and bake for another 8 min or until the crust is very lightly browned. Cool on wire rack.

For Sour Cream Pumpkin Pie:

Increase oven heat to 450F. Centre oven rack. Line a baking sheet with parchment paper and put a pie plate on it.

Into a food processor, combine all filling ingredients and process for about 2 min, scrape down the sides of the bowl twice. Pour the filling into the crust.

Bake for about 10 min, then reduce the oven heat to 300F, continue baking for another 40 min or until a toothpick inserted comes out clean. Transfer onto a rack to cool.

Serve with whipped cream.

Pumpkin Orange Pie

This Creamy Orange Pumpkin Pie has the ability to indulge anyone into its creamy, zesty taste.

Ingredients

- 1 frozen deep dish pie shell, 9 inch, baked
- 1 cup of white sugar
- 1 tablespoon of gelatine, un-flavoured
- 1 teaspoon of pumpkin pie spice
- 1/2 teaspoon of salt
- 13 ounces of evaporated milk
- 2 whole eggs, separated
- 1/2 cup of orange marmalade
- 1/2 cup of pecans, chopped

Directions

Into a saucepan, combine 1/2 cup sugar, gelatine, pumpkin pie spice and salt; stir and add evaporated milk. Bring to boil while stirring. Put off heat.

Into a bowl, beat egg yolks. Pour some hot mixture, stir and pour back into the saucepan. Mix well, heat again with stirring, until mixture thickens. Remove from heat. Stir in pumpkin and orange marmalade.

Chill until mixture firms.

Into a bowl, whisk egg whites until foamy; slowly beat in remaining sugar until dissolved and stiff peaks form; fold into pumpkin mixture.

Pour into prepared pie shell and top with pecans or coconut flakes. Chill before serving.

Crustless Pumpkin Pie

This is a delicious, pumpkin pie made a little healthier by eliminating the excess fat and calories of a crust. This is always a treat dessert and a wise alternative to a traditional pie.

Ingredients

Brown Sugar Topping

¼ cup of rolled oats

¼ cup of brown sugar

1 tablespoon of butter, softened

½ teaspoon of cinnamon

Pie

15 ounces of canned pumpkin puree

12 ounces of evaporated skim milk

½ cup of brown sugar

2 eggs

½ cup of flour

1 teaspoon of baking powder

2 teaspoons of pumpkin pie spice

1 teaspoon of cinnamon

Directions

Preheat the oven to 350F. Grease a 9-inch pie pan.

The Brown Sugar Topping: Into a bowl, mix brown sugar, oats and cinnamon until blended. Set aside.

Mix evaporated milk, pumpkin, sugar and eggs into a large mixing bowl until well combined.

Into another bowl, combine the baking powder, flour, pumpkin pie spice and cinnamon; mix well. Gradually add to pumpkin mixture and fold until well combined.

Pour pumpkin pie mixture into your prepared pie plate. Sprinkle the Brown Sugar Topping and bake for about 55 min. Cool outside oven for about 10 min, and then move to the fridge for at least 4 - 6 hrs.

Pecan Pumpkin Pie

The tasty, crunchy pecan topping and maple syrup provide a delectable twist to creamy pumpkin pie.

Ingredients

1 – 9 inch pie shell, prepared

2 eggs

15 ounces of canned pumpkin puree

½ cup of maple syrup

¼ cup of white sugar

¼ cup of heavy whipping cream

1 ½ teaspoons of ground cinnamon

1 teaspoon of ground nutmeg

TOPPING:

2 eggs, beaten

1 cup of chopped pecans

½ cup of white sugar

½ cup of maple syrup

Topping – whipped topping, optional

Directions

Preheat oven to 425F.

Into a large mixing bowl, whip eggs, with the rest of the ingredient, until smooth; pour the pie batter into prepared pie crust.

Prepare the topping: Into another large mixing bowl, combine pecans, eggs, sugar and syrup; mix well. Scoop all over the top and bake for about 15 min. Reduce the oven to 350° and bake further for 45 min or until the pie is set and crust is golden brown.

Transfer pie to a wire rack and cool for 60 minutes. Chill overnight. Serve with whipped topping.

Pumpkin Bourbon Pie

A hint of bourbon and whipped cream in the filling adds delight to this pumpkin pie.

Ingredients

- 3/4 cup of packed light brown sugar
- 1 teaspoon of ground cinnamon
- 1/2 teaspoon of salt
- 1/2 teaspoon of ground ginger
- 1/4 teaspoon of ground cloves
- 2 whole eggs
- 1 (15 ounces) can of pure pumpkin
- 1 (12 fluid ounces) can of evaporated milk
- 2 tablespoons of bourbon
- 1 deep-dish pie shell, 9-inch

Bourbon whipped cream

- 1 cup of heavy cream
- 2 tablespoons of light brown sugar

2 teaspoons of bourbon

1 teaspoon of ground ginger

Directions

Preheat oven to 425F.

Into a bowl, whisk sugar, cinnamon, salt, ginger and cloves; until blended.

Into another bowl, whip eggs. Stir in pumpkin and sugar-spice mixture. Slowly stir in evaporated milk and bourbon. Spread into prepared pie shell.

Bake for 15 min. Reduce oven heat to 350F and bake further for about 45 min or until toothpick inserted comes out clean. Cool on wire rack for 2 hours. Serve at once with Bourbon Whipped Cream or chill to store.

Prepare bourbon whipped cream. Into a large mixer bowl, whip 1 cup heavy cream until soft peaks form. Add 2 tablespoons light brown sugar, 2 teaspoons bourbon and 1 teaspoon ground ginger; continue to whip until stiff peaks form

Pumpkin Rum Pie

Ingredients

1-9 inch premade pie shell
15 ounces of canned pumpkin puree
3 eggs
1cup of brown sugar
2 tablespoons of butter, melted
1 ½ cups of heavy cream
1/3 cup of sour cream
2 teaspoons of cinnamon
2 teaspoons of ginger
¼ teaspoon of cloves
¼ teaspoon of nutmeg
¼ teaspoon of salt
3 tablespoons of dark rum
2 teaspoons of vanilla

Directions:

Preheat your oven to 375 degrees.

In a large mixing bowl, bear together the eggs, pumpkin, brown sugar, butter and the heavy cream until well combined. Bear in the sour cream. Now beat in the spices, salt, vanilla and the rum.

Pour pie batter into pie crust and bake for 10 minutes. Reduce the heat to 300 degrees and bake for an additional 40 – 45 minutes. Cool on a wire cooling rack and then store in fridge until you are ready to serve.

Apple Pumpkin Pie

This fruity pumpkin pie has a scrumptious layer of apples underneath the pumpkin.

Ingredients

　1/3 cup of brown sugar

　1 teaspoon of ground cinnamon

　1 tablespoon of corn starch

　½ teaspoon of salt

　1/3 cup of water

　3 tablespoons of butter, melted

　3 cups of apples, sliced, peeled

　1 9 inch prepared pie shell

Pumpkin Layer

　¾ cup of canned pumpkin

　¾ cup of evaporated milk

　1/3 cup of sugar

　1 egg

1 teaspoon of ground cinnamon

½ teaspoon of salt

Topping - Whipped cream, optional

Directions

Preheat oven to 375F.

Combine in a saucepan sugar, cinnamon, corn starch, and salt. Stir in water until smooth. Add the butter and bring to a boil over medium heat. Stir in apples and cook for 4 min or until tender.

Spread apple mixture into the pastry placed in a 9-in. pie plate.

Into a bowl, combine all ingredients for the pumpkin layer and whisk until smooth; pour all over apple layer. Trim and groove the edges of the crust.

Bake for nearly 53 min or until toothpick inserted comes out clean. Cool completely and top with the whipped cream for serving.

Pumpkin Dutch Apple Pie

Apples and Pumpkins are two of the most wonderful dessert flavours – especially in the fall months. Why not combine these tastes in this delicious crisp pie?

Ingredients

1 9 inch deep dish pastry shell

Apple Layer

2 teaspoons of flour

2 cups of apples, peeled, cored, thinly sliced

¼ cup of sugar

1 teaspoon of lemon juice

½ teaspoon of ground cinnamon

Pumpkin Layer

1 ½ cups of canned pure pumpkin

3 tablespoons of butter, softened

1 teaspoon of ground cinnamon

1 cup of evaporated milk

1/2 cup of granulated sugar

2 eggs, lightly beaten

½ teaspoon of salt

¼ teaspoon of ground nutmeg

Crumble topping

½ cup of flour

½ cup of chopped walnuts

6 tablespoons of granulated sugar

4 tablespoons of butter, melted

Directions

Preheat oven to 375F. Press pie shell into pie pan.

Prepare apple layer. Into a bowl, combine all ingredients; mix well and spread into prepared pie shell.

Prepare pumpkin layer. Into the same bowl, combine all ingredients, whisk until blended. Pour all over the apple layer. Bake initially for 30 min before topping the crumbs.

Prepare the crumb topping. Into the same bowl, mix flour, sugar and nuts. Cut in butter and mix until crumbly. Sprinkle over the half-baked pastry and bake for another 20 min or until set. Cool totally on wire rack.

Pumpkin Mousse Pie

The fluffed filling in this luscious pie forms nutmeg-coloured lovely peaks. Rich and creamy, this widely- held dessert tastes so delicious with its buttery graham cracker crust.

Ingredients

- 1-1/2 cups of graham cracker crumbs
- 1/4 cup of packed brown sugar
- 6 tablespoons of butter, softened

Filling

- 1 (15 ounces) can of pumpkin
- 1 (7 ounces) jar of marshmallow creme
- 1/4 cup of packed brown sugar
- 2 teaspoons of pumpkin pie spice
- 1 (12 ounces) carton of frozen whipped topping, thawed, divided

Directions

Preheat oven to 350F. Lightly grease a 9-in pie plate.

Into a bowl, combine the cracker crumbs, sugar and butter; mix until incorporated. Pat onto the bottom and up the sides of prepared pie plate and bake for about 8 min or until lightly browned. Cool completely on a wire rack.

Prepare filling. Into a large bowl, whisk all the ingredients. Fold in 3-1/2 cups of whipped topping and spread into prepared crust; cover and freeze for at least 4 hrs. or until firm. Garnish with remaining whipped topping.

Double Layer Pumpkin Pie

One will be treated with a double flavour and colour in this double Layered Pumpkin Pie that is beautiful yet delicious.

Ingredients

- 1 preready graham cracker pie crust, 8-inch
- 4 ounces of cream cheese, softened
- 1 tablespoon of evaporated milk, chilled
- 1 tablespoon of sugar
- 1 ½ cups of frozen whipped topping, thawed
- 1 cup of evaporated milk, chilled
- 2 (3.4 oz.) packs of vanilla instant pudding & pie filling mix
- 15 ounces of canned pumpkin
- 1 ½ teaspoon of ground cinnamon
- 1 teaspoon of ground ginger
- ½ teaspoon of ground cloves
- Topping – whipped cream topping

Directions

Into a large bowl combine 1 tablespoon of evaporated milk, cream cheese and sugar, beat until smooth. Gradually stir in whipped topping. Spread pie mixture onto the bottom of prepared pie crust.

Into a mixing bowl, combine 1 cup of evaporated milk and pudding mixes. Beat with wire whisk for 1 minute. Stir in pumpkin and spices until well mixed. Spread all over cream cheese layer.

Chill pie in fridge for about 4 hrs. or until firm. Garnish with additional whipped topping if desired.

Chocolate Pumpkin Pie

Two kinds of delicious chocolates, plus marshmallows are enough to drive anyone crazy for this sweet delight that's perfect for any occasion – big or small.

Ingredients

1 cup of pumpkin puree

2 cups of marshmallows, chopped

8 ounces of milk chocolate chips

8 ounces of miniature semisweet chocolate chips

12 ounces of frozen whipped topping, thawed

1 graham cracker crust, 9-in

Plus mini chocolate chips, optional, for garnish

Directions

Into a large microwavable bowl, combine marshmallows, pumpkin and chocolate chips. Heat, uncovered, for 1 minute on high; stir and heat for another 30 sec or until marshmallows are melted and mixture is well blended. Continue microwaving, stirring every 15 seconds, until all ingredients are melted. Cool to room temperature, stirring a number of times.

Reserve about 1 – 2 tablespoons of whipped topping and fold remaining topping into pumpkin mixture. Spread it into prepared crust and top pie with the reserved whipped topping and the mini chips. Chill for at least 3 - 4 hrs. then slice to serve.

Spiced Pumpkin Pie

The smooth and creamy filling is bursting with a wonderful blend of spices, a perfect pumpkin pie for any Thanksgiving.

Ingredients

- 3 eggs, lightly beaten
- 1 cup of milk
- ½ cup of white sugar
- ½ cup of brown sugar
- 1 ½ teaspoons of cinnamon
- 1 teaspoon of nutmeg
- 1 teaspoon of salt
- 1 teaspoon of ground ginger
- 1 teaspoon of ground cloves
- 15 ounces of pumpkin puree
- 1 9 inch pastry shell
- Topping - Frozen Whipped topping cinnamon

Directions

Preheat oven to 350F.

Into a large mixing bowl, mix together the milk, eggs, sugars, spices and salt. Stir in pumpkin just until blended. Pour into your prepared pastry shell.

Bake for about 55 min or until toothpick inserted comes out clean. Cool on wire cooking rack. Garnish the pie with the whipped topping, the sprinkle more cinnamon on top and chill before serving.

Gingersnap Pumpkin Pie

Enjoy this delicious and decadent gingersnap pumpkin pie. A great recipe for special occasions and holidays.

Ingredients

Crust

- 2 cups of gingersnap cookie crumbs, finely ground
- 2 tablespoons of sugar
- 1/3 cup of butter, melted

Filling

- 2 envelopes of unflavoured gelatine
- ¼ cup of hot water
- 2/3 cup of evaporated milk
- 30 ounces of pumpkin puree
- 1 (3.4 oz.) box of vanilla instant pudding and pie filling mix
- 1 ½ teaspoons of pumpkin pie spice
- 1 ½ cups of frozen whipped topping, thawed

Directions

Preheat the oven to 350F. Lightly grease a deep dish pie pan, 9 inches.

Into a large mixing bowl, combine sugar and crumbs; mix well. Cut in butter, mix until crumbly. Set aside 1/3 cup of crumb mixture as topping. Pat the remaining crumb mixture onto the bottom of the pie plate and up sides of prepared pie plate. Bake for about 8 min and cool totally on wire rack.

Prepare filling. Into a small saucepan, mix gelatine and water; let stand for 1 min. Heat over low heat, stirring frequently, until dissolved. Stir in milk; heat, stirring often, until just hot. Put off heat.

Into a large mixer bowl and using hand mixer, beat, pudding, pumpkin, evaporated milk & gelatine mixture and the pumpkin pie spice on high for 3 min. Gradually Fold in the whipped topping. Spread pumpkin pie mixture into crumb crust and drizzle with reserved crumb mixture. Chill for 3 – 4 hours or until firm enough to slice.

Pumpkin Chiffon Pie

The vanilla pudding makes this pumpkin chiffon pie extra creamy.

Ingredients

3 ounces of cream cheese, softened

1 tablespoon of sugar

1-1/2 cups of whipped topping

1 graham cracker crust, 9 inches

1 cup of cold milk

2 (3.4 ounces) packs of instant vanilla pudding mix

15 ounces of canned pumpkin puree

1 ½ teaspoons of cinnamon

1 teaspoon of ginger

½ teaspoon of cloves

Topping – frozen topping and chopped pecans

Directions

In a large mixing bowl, beat together the sugar and cream cheese until smooth. Gradually Add the whipped topping and mix well. Spread pie filling into crust.

In another mixing bowl, beat pudding mixes and milk together on low speed until well combined for 2 – 3 minutes. Let stand for 3 - 5 minutes. Stir in the pumpkin puree and all the spices; mix well. Spread the pumpkin mixture over cream cheese layer. Chill. If desired, Garnish with additional frozen topping and sprinkle nuts on top.

No-Bake Pumpkin Pie

What makes a no-bake cake so delicious and nutritious? It's the light creams and sugar-free vanilla pudding that makes all the difference.

Ingredients

4 ounces of lite cream cheese

1 tablespoon of milk

1 (8 oz.) pack of lite cool whip

1 prepared graham crust, 9-inch

1 (16oz.) can of pumpkin

1 cup of milk

13/4 teaspoon of pumpkin pie spice

1(1 kg.) pack of sugar-free vanilla pudding mix

Directions

Into a large bowl, whisk cream cheese and milk until smooth. Gradually stir in 11/2 cup of the cool whip, spread on bottom of prepared crust.

Into large bowl, combine 1 cup milk, pumpkin and the spice, stir well to blend. Add in pudding, mix well and spread all over the cream cheese layer. Chill it for about 4 hrs. and top with remaining cool whip.

Pumpkin Ice Cream Pie

This attractive layered pumpkin pie is so easy to make and prepare with the convenience of canned pumpkin and ready to-eat candy bars.

Ingredients

- 3 toffee candy bars, crushed, divided
- 3 cups of vanilla bean ice cream, softened, divided
- 1 chocolate crumb pie crust, 9 inches
- ½ cup of canned pumpkin
- 2 tablespoons of sugar
- 1 teaspoon of ground cinnamon
- ½ teaspoon of ground nutmeg

Directions

Combine together 2 of the crushed candy bars and 2 cups of the vanilla bean ice cream. Spoon this mixture into the chocolate pie crust and chill in freezer for at least 1 hour, until firm.

Into a large mixing bowl, combine sugar, pumpkin, spices and remaining ice cream. Scoop the pumpkin mixture onto the first ice cream layer and then sprinkle with remaining crushed toffee candy bars. Cover and freeze for at least 12 hours before serving. Good to store and eat for 2 months.

Remove from the freezer 15 - 20 minutes before serving, in order to soften. Run knife under warm or hot water to make slicing this ice cream pie easier.

Praline Pumpkin Pie

The pecan rich buttery crust and spiced pumpkin filling made this pie a real treat.

Ingredients

1/3 cup of packed brown sugar

3 tablespoons of butter, melted

1/3 cup of pecans, finely chopped

1 unbaked pastry shell, 10 inches

Filling:

3 whole eggs, lightly beaten

1/2 cup of white sugar

1/2 cup of packed brown sugar

2 tablespoons of all-purpose flour

3/4 teaspoon of ground cinnamon

1/2 teaspoon of salt

1/2 teaspoon of ground ginger

1/4 teaspoon of ground cloves

1 (15 ounces) can of solid-pack pumpkin

1-1/2 cups of half-and-half cream

Additional chopped pecans, optional

Directions

Preheat oven to 450F.

Into a small bowl, combine sugar, pecans and butter; until crumbly. Pat onto the bottom of prepared pie shell. Perforate sides of pastry using a fork and bake for about 10 min. Cool on a wire rack. Reduce oven temperature to 350F.

Prepare the filling. In a large bowl, whisk eggs, sugar, flour and spices; stir in pumpkin. Slowly add cream, mix to blend. Pour into baked pastry shell and return to oven for another 48 min of baking or until a toothpick inserted comes out clean. Cool on a wire rack. Chill for at least 3 hrs. before serving.

Frozen Pumpkin Pie

This classic pumpkin pie got a real twist with vanilla ice cream enriched filling.

Ingredients

- 1 quart of French vanilla ice cream, melted
- 1 teaspoon of ground cinnamon
- ¾ cup of canned pumpkin puree
- ½ teaspoon of ground ginger
- ½ cup of honey
- ¼ teaspoon of nutmeg
- ¼ teaspoon of cloves
- ¼ teaspoon of salt
- 1 graham cracker crust, 9 inches
- Topping – whipped topping and toasted pecans

Directions

In a large mixing bowl combine pumpkin, salt, honey and spices. Stir in French vanilla ice cream. Beat until smooth. Spread pie filling into prepared graham cracker crust. Cover pie and place in freezer for 2 – 4 hours.

Remove from the freezer 15 - 20 minutes before serving. Garnish with whipped topping and toasted pecans.

Cheese Pumpkin Swirl Pie

Pumpkin puree mixed with cream cheese creates a delicious and creamy, but attractive dessert.

Ingredients

- 1 – 9 inch deep-dish pie shell
- 3 ounces of cream cheese, melted
- ½ cup of corn syrup, divided
- 1 teaspoon of vanilla
- 1 cup of canned pumpkin
- ½ cup of evaporated milk
- 2 eggs, lightly beaten
- ¼ cup of sugar
- 2 teaspoons of pumpkin pie spice
- ½ teaspoon of salt

Directions

Preheat your oven to 325F.

Into small mixing bowl beat the cream cheese until light and fluffy. Gradually add 1/4 cup corn syrup and the vanilla extract; beat together until smooth.

Into a medium mixing bowl, combine the rest of the corn syrup and the remaining ingredients. Pour pie batter into your prepared pie shell and drop the cream cheese mixture by tablespoonful portions onto pumpkin filling. Whirl mixture with spoon or a butter knife, pulling pumpkin mixture up to surface.

Bake for about 55 - 60 min or until toothpick inserted comes out clean. Cool completely on wire rack.

Pumpkin Cream Cheese Pie

A luscious dessert; made from creamy cheesy crust and creamy spiced pumpkin filling.

Ingredients

1 (8 ounces) package cream cheese, melted

3 tablespoons of powdered sugar

1 teaspoon of vanilla

1 – 9 inch unbaked pastry shell

FILLING:

2 cups of heavy whipping cream

1 ½ cups of pumpkin puree

2 eggs, lightly beaten

¾ cup of white sugar

2 teaspoons of pumpkin pie spice

Directions

Preheat oven to 350F.

Into a large mixing bowl, whisk together sugar, cream cheese and vanilla until smooth and creamy. Spread this mixture into prepared pastry shell.

Into a separate mixing bowl, combine all filling ingredients; mix until smooth. Pour all over the botom layer. Cover pie with foil, loosely, and bake for about 1 hour and 15 minutes or until a toothpick inserted comes out clean. Cool on a wire rack.

Pumpkin Hazelnut Pie

This is a sweet and delicious version of the classic pumpkin pie – the hazelnut topping adds some crunch to the already creamy and tasty pumpkin pie.

Ingredients

Crust

2 cups of flour

2 tablespoons of confectioners' sugar

1 teaspoon of salt

¾ cup of butter, cubed

6 tablespoons of ice water

1 teaspoon of white vinegar

Filling

3 eggs, lightly beaten

15 ounces of canned pumpkin

¾ cup of brown sugar

½ cup of sour cream

3 tablespoons of 3 flour

3 tablespoons of hazelnut liqueur3

3 teaspoons of pumpkin pie spice

Topping

¼ cup of brown sugar

2 tablespoons of flour

3 tablespoons of butter

½ cup of hazelnuts, chopped

1 tablespoon of hazelnut liqueur

Directions

Pie Dough: Into a bowl, combine flour with salt and sugar; mix well. Cut in butter and mix until crumbly. Slowly add in mixture of vinegar and water, mixing after every addition, until dough forms. Wrap in plastic and chill for 30 min or until firm.

Roll out dough and fit into a 9-in. pie plate. Trim and flute edges.

Pie Filling: Into another bowl, combine all the pumpkin pie filling ingredients and then mix them together until blended. Pour into crust.

Pie Topping: Into a small bowl, combine flour and brown sugar. Cut in butter and mix until crumbly. Stir in liqueur and the chopped hazelnuts; sprinkle over filling. Cover edges loosely with foil and bake for about 53 min or until a toothpick inserted comes out clean. Cool on a wire rack.

Almond Pumpkin Pie

If you are looking for a pumpkin pie that offers a different flavour and you want a little crunch to your holiday pie, look no further.

Ingredients

1 deep-dish pie shell, 9-inch

1/3 cup of almonds, slivered, finely chopped, toasted

1 egg, lightly beaten

1 cup canned pumpkin puree

1/2 cup of sugar

1 ½ teaspoons of pumpkin pie spice

2/3 cup of corn syrup

2 eggs, lightly beaten

½ cup of sugar

3 tablespoons of butter, melted

½ teaspoon of almond extract

1 cup slivered almonds, toasted

Directions

Preheat oven to 350F. Press fit unbaked shell into 9-in pie pan.

Prepare crust by pressing almonds all over the bottom.

Into a medium bowl, whisk 1/3 cup sugar, pumpkin, egg and pumpkin pie spice Spread all over the bottom of prepared deep dish pie shell.

Into the same bowl, mix 2 eggs, corn syrup, butter, remaining sugar and almond extract and stir in remaining almonds. Scoop it all over the pumpkin layer and bake for about 53 min or until filling is set. Cool on wire rack

Apple Butter Pumpkin Pie

Enjoy the marriage of apples and pumpkins like never before in this delicious pie!

Ingredients

1 cup of pumpkin puree

½ cup of brown sugar

1 cup of apple butter

1 teaspoon of ground cinnamon

1 teaspoon of ground nutmeg

½ teaspoon of ground ginger

1 teaspoon of salt

3 eggs, lightly beaten

¾ cup of evaporated milk

1 – 9 inch unbaked pastry shell

Topping - Whipped cream

Directions

Preheat oven to 425F. Press fit unbaked shell into 9-in pie pan.

Into a mixing bowl, combine the pumpkin, sugar apple butter, cinnamon, nutmeg, ginger and salt. Beat in eggs. Gradually mix in milk until smooth. Spread into prepared pastry shell.

Cover edges loosely with foil and bake for about 38 min or until set. Remove foil and reduce temperature to 400F and bake for another 7 min. or until golden brown. Cool on a wire rack.

Top the pie with whipped cream. Refrigerate leftovers.

Mini Pumpkin Pies

Pumpkin pies made handier and tastier.

Ingredients

4 – 4 inch mini pie crusts

1 cup of sugar

1 teaspoon of salt

1 ½ teaspoons of ground cinnamon

1 teaspoon of ground ginger

½ teaspoon of ground cloves

2 eggs

15 ounces of canned pumpkin

12 ounces of evaporated milk

Directions

Preheat your oven to 425F.

Combine salt, sugar and spices in a small mixing bowl; mix well. Into a large mixing bowl, beat the eggs lightly. Add sugar and spice mixture. Gradually mix in evaporated milk. Stir in Pumpkin Puree.

Beat eggs lightly into a large bowl; mix in pumpkin and sugar-spice mixture. Slowly stir in evaporated milk and pour into pie shells.

Bake for 15 min. Reduce oven temperature to 350F and bake further for 35 - 40 min or until toothpick or fork inserted in center of pies come out clean. Cool on wire rack. Serve immediately or chill to store.

Pumpkin Caramel-Crunch Pie

The addition of whipping cream and chopped walnuts made this pie both creamy and crunchy.

Ingredients

- ¾ cup of brown sugar, divided
- ¼ cup of walnuts, finely chopped
- 3 tablespoons of butter, softened
- 1 – 9 inch pastry shell
- 3 eggs
- 1 cup of pumpkin puree
- 1 ½ teaspoons of rum extract
- 1 ½ teaspoons of cinnamon
- 1 teaspoon of salt
- ½ teaspoon of ginger
- 1 ½ cups of heavy whipping cream
- Toppings – frozen whipped topping and additional chopped walnuts

Directions

Preheat oven to 400F. Press unbaked shell into 9-in pie pan.

Into a small mixing bowl, combine butter, walnuts and ¼ cup of brown sugar and mix until crumbly. Press this crunchy mixture onto the bottom of the pastry shell.

Into a large mixing bowl, whisk together the eggs with the remaining brown sugar. Mix in the pumpkin puree, salt and the spices until blended; fold in the heavy cream.

Spread the pie filling into the prepared pastry shell. Loosely cover edges with foil and bake for about 10 min. Reduce oven temp. to 350° and bake for 45 min longer or until a toothpick inserted comes out clean. Remove the foil. Cool the pie on a wire rack. If desired, top the pie with whipped cream and additional walnuts.

Maple Pumpkin Pie

This may be a version of pumpkin pie that you have not tried before. Take the risk, you will glad you did!

Ingredients

2 eggs

15 ounces of pumpkin puree

1 cup of evaporated milk

1 cup of sugar

½ cup of maple syrup

2 teaspoons of pumpkin pie spice

½ teaspoon of salt

9 inch prepared pie crust

Maple whipped cream:

1 cup of heavy whipping cream

3 tablespoons of powdered sugar

1 ½ tablespoon of maple syrup

½ teaspoon of pumpkin pie spice

Toasted and chopped pecans

Directions

Preheat oven to 425F. Prepare pie shell and set aside.

Into a large mixing bowl, combine the mix together the pumpkin puree, milk, sugar and maple syrup until well blended. Stire in the eggs, salt and pumpkin pie spice. Pour pie filling into prepared crust.

Bake for about 15 minutes in preheated oven. Reduce the temp. to 350F and bake for an additional 45 – 50 min longer or until crust is golden brown and top of pie is set. Cool on a wire rack and chill overnight or until firm.

Into a small mixing bowl, whisk together the maple whipped cream ingredients until firm crests form. Scoop onto pie and drizzle with pecans.

Upside Down Pumpkin Pie Cake

Okay – so not exactly a pie. But if you are looking for a good alternative to the pumpkin pie or something to serve in addition to the traditional pumpkin pie, this is a good and simple choice.

Ingredients

    3 cups of pumpkin puree
    3 eggs
    1 cup of sugar
    3 tablespoons of pumpkin pie spice
    13 ounces of evaporated milk
    1 box of white or yellow cake mix
    ¾ cup of butter

Directions

Preheat oven to 350F. Lightly grease a 13 x 9-in baking pan.

Combine the first five ingredients in a large mixing bowl and then pour into prepared pan. Sprinkle the cake mix over the pumpkin mixture.

Melt the butter and then pour it over cake mix and bake for about an hour in preheated oven or until set.

When you are ready to serve the cake, use a butter knife to loosen the cake from the baking dish and then turn it upside down on a serving platter. Can be topped with frozen whipped topping and nuts.

Tofu Pumpkin Pie

Looking for a healthy alternative for pumpkin pie? Try this delicious recipe for tofu pumpkin pie today!

Ingredients

2 cups of granola cereal, crumbled
½ cup of whole wheat flour
1 cup of coconut, shredded
½ cup of apple juice concentrate
1 pound firm tofu, drained

15 ounces of pumpkin puree
2 teaspoons of pure vanilla extract
½ cup of honey
½ cup of pure maple syrup
2 tablespoon of pumpkin pie spice

Directions

Preheat oven to 375F. Grease a 9-in pie pan.

Into a bowl combine cereal, whole wheat flour, coconut and juice concentrate. Mix until well blended. Press onto the bottom and up to the sides of pie dish. Bake for 8 - 10 min or until golden brown. Cool completely. Reduce oven to 350 degrees.

Into a bowl of a mixer, combine the rest of the ingredients, blend until smooth. Spread into the 9-inch pie crust and bake for about an hour. Cool for a while. Chill before serving.

Pumpkin Pie with Pecan Brittle Topping

Yummy Homemade Pumpkin Pie with Pecan Brittle Topping - adds a new flavor experience to this wonderful pumpkin dessert.

Ingredients

For the filling

1 (15 ounce) can of pumpkin puree
¾ cup of milk
½ teaspoon of salt
1 teaspoon of vanilla extract
¼ cup of brown sugar
2/3 cup of pure maple syrup
3 whole eggs, beaten
1 piecrust, 9 inches

For the Pecan Brittle

¼ cup of water

¾ cup of white granulated sugar

1/8 teaspoon of salt

¾ cup of toasted chopped pecans

Directions

Preheat oven to 375F. Press fit unbaked shell into 9-in pie pan. Line a baking sheet with tin foil, spray non-stick oil.

Into a bowl, combine the first six ingredients; mix well. Beat in egg. Spread into prepared pie crust. Loosely cover edges with tin foil and bake for about 30 min. Remove foil and continue baking for another 25 min. Cool then chill for 2 hrs.

Into a saucepan, heat water and stir in sugar to dissolve. Bring to a boil over medium heat until amber colored. Put off heat. Stir in pecans. Spread into prepared baking sheet. Drizzle salt. Cool and chill to firm. Break into small pieces and top onto the pie.

Pumpkin Banana Meringue Pies

Ingredients

2 cups of all-purpose flour
1/4 cup of icing sugar mixture
¾ cup of chilled butter, chopped
1 egg yolk
15 ounces of pumpkin puree
2 teaspoons of pumpkin pie spice
2 tablespoon of iced water
1/3 cup of caramel
1 large banana, peeled, sliced
2 egg whites
1/4 cup of caster sugar

Direction

Preheat oven to 400F. Line four 1 x 3-inch round fluted tart tin.

Into the bowl of a food processor, combine flour, icing sugar and butter, process until crumbly. Add egg yolk, and water, beat until dough is formed. Work the dough and form into a disk, wrap and chill for 30 min.

Divide dough into four equal portions. Roll each portion into 1/8-in thick disk and fit into bottom and up the sides of prepared tin pans. Cover and chill for 15 min.

Press liners into the crusts and put baking weights. Place on baking sheet and bake for about 10 min or until light brown. Cool slightly. Reduce oven heat to 350F.

Removed from tart tins and set aside.

In a small mixing bowl combine the pumpkin puree and the pumpkin pie spice. Pour the pumpkin filling evenly into each tart tin. Top with caramel and then sliced bananas.

Prepare glaze. Into a bowl, whisk egg whites until firm crests form. Gradually add sugar, whisking until smooth and glossy. Spoon it all over tarts and bake for 5 min or until golden. Cool then serve.

Pumpkin Meringue Pie

Ingredients

1 1/2 cup of canned pumpkin, mashed

1/2 cup of white sugar

1 teaspoon of cinnamon, ground

1/4 teaspoon of nutmeg, ground

1/4 teaspoon of cloves, ground

1/2 teaspoon of salt

3 whole eggs, separated

1 cup of evaporated milk

1 unbaked pie shell, 9-inch

1/8 teaspoon of salt

6 tablespoon of sugar

Direction

Preheat oven to 400F. Press fit unbaked shell into 9-in pie pan.

Into a bowl, combine pumpkin, sugar, spices, and salt; mix well. Beat in egg yolks until blended. Slowly mix in milk. Spread into pie shell and bake for about 35 min. until a toothpick inserted comes out clean. Heat up oven to

425F.

Make the meringue. Into a bowl, whisk egg whites and 1/8 tsp. salt until foamy. Gradually add sugar, whisking after every addition until glossy and firm. Liberally spoon it all over the top of warm pie. Create soft peak at the center and bake for about 5 min. until light browned. Cool on a wire rack

Coconut Pumpkin Pie

This pumpkin pie is so scrumptious, healthy, nutritious and fiber- packed.

Ingredients

1 frozen 9 inch deep dish pie crust

3 eggs, beaten

3/4 cup of brown sugar

2 tablespoons of pumpkin pie spice

1 teaspoon of salt

15 ounces of pumpkin puree

14 ounces of coconut milk

Directions

Preheat oven to 425F.

Into a large mixing bowl, whisk together the eggs, pumpkin pie spice, sugar and salt until smooth and creamy. Stir in the pumpkin puree and gradually add the coconut milk, mix until well blended. Pour pie filling into pie crust.

Bake for about 15 min. Reduce oven heat to 350F and bake for another 45 - 50 min or until toothpick inserted into center of the pie comes out clean. Cool on wire rack.

Custard Pumpkin Pie

Here is another great variation of the typical pumpkin pie.

Ingredients

2 cups of canned pumpkin
1 cup of sugar
1 teaspoon of salt
1 ½ teaspoons of ground cinnamon
1 teaspoon of ginger
1 teaspoon of nutmeg
2 eggs, beaten
1 cup of heavy whipping cream
½ cup of whole milk
1 – 9 in deep dish pie shell, unbaked

Direction

Preheat your oven to 400F. Press fit unbaked shell into 9-in pie pan.

Into a saucepan, heat the pumpkin puree over medium-high heat for 10 - 12 min or until slightly dried and caramelized.

Pull from heat and mix in sugar, salt and spices until well blended. Beat in the eggs, cream and the milk. Mix until smooth and spread pie filling into prepared pie shell.

Bake it for about 25 - 30 min or until crust is golden brown. Cool completely on wire rack before slicing.

Top with whipped cream if desired.

Pumpkin Squash Pie

For a true autumn treat, serve this wonderfully delicious pie that combines the flavors of squash and pumpkin in one tasty dessert.

Ingredients

1 premade pie crust

2 small pumpkins, cut into wedges

2 small squashes, cut into wedges

olive oil, for drizzling

3 eggs plus 2 legg yolks

1 cup of heavy cream

½ cup of dark-brown sugar

3 tablespoons of brandy

1 ½ tablespoons of fresh sage

2 teaspoons of cinnamon

1 ½ teaspoons of ginger

½ teaspoon of allspice

¼ teaspoon of cloves

¼ teaspoon of nutmeg

1 teaspoon of Salt

¼ teaspoon of freshly ground pepper

Topping – frozen whipped topping

Directions

Preheat your oven to 375F.

On a baking sheet, spread out the squash and the pumpkin wedges. Drizzle olive oil on the pumpkin and squash and roast until tender.

Peel toasted squash and pumpkin, and puree in a food processor until smooth. Transfer into a bowl and add in egg yolks, whole eggs, heavy cream, brandy, brown sugar, spices, salt and pepper. Whisk to combine.

Pour and smooth the pie filling into the prepared pie shell, and bake for about an hour until just set but still slightly shaky in the center. Let cool on a wire rack.

You can serve this pie chilled, slightly warm or topped with whipped cream (warm or cold

Sweet Potato Pumpkin Pie

Enjoy this delicious sweet potato pie with some subtle pumpkin taste. Delicious.

Ingredients:
1 premade pie crust
15 ounces of pumpkin puree
1 cup of sweet potatoes, mashed
1 cup of brown sugar
2 teaspoons of cinnamon
1 teaspoon of salt
1 teaspoon of ginger
1 teaspoon of nutmeg
½ teaspoon of cloves
3 beaten eggs
1 ¼ cups of heavy cream
5 ounces of evaporated milk
1 ½ teaspoons of dark rum
2 cups of pecans, halved
½ of brown sugar
1/4 cup of heavy cream
Frozen whipped topping

Directions

Preheat oven to 400 degrees.

In a large mixing bowl combine the canned pumpkin, sweet potatoes, 1 cup of brown sugar, salt and spices, mix well. Stir in the eggs, 1 ¼ cup of heavy cream, milk and the dark rum until well combined. Pour pie filling into pie crust.

Bake pie in preheated oven for 45 minutes. Cool on wire rack.

Turn oven down to 350 degrees.

To make sugared pecans take a small mixing bowl and combine the pecan halves, sugar and cream. Spread this mixture into a greased baking pan which is 15 x 10 x 1 inches. Bake in preheated oven for 20 – 25 minutes until the pecans are toasted. Cool pecans.

Once the pecans are cooled, top the pie with them.

Serve pie with a dallop of whipped cream on top.

Decadent Chocolate Pumpkin Pie

Ingredients:

1 premade chocolate cookie pie crust
6 ounces of semisweet baking chocolate, chopped
2 ounces of cold butter, chopped
15 ounces of pumpkin puree
12 ounces of evaporated milk
1 cup of brown sugar
3 eggs
1 tablespoon of cornstarch
2 teaspoons of vanilla
1 teaspoon of salt
1 ½ teaspoons of cinnamon
1 ½ teaspoons of ginger
½ teaspoon of nutmeg
¼ teaspoon of cloves

Topping:
1 ½ ounces of milk chocolate, melted
Frozen whipped cream

Directions:

In a microwave safe bowl, melt the semisweet chocolate and the butter together. Stir every 30 seconds until the butter chocolate mixture is smooth. Set aside.

In a large mixing bowl combine milk, pumpkin puree, brown sugar, eggs, cornstarch, vanilla extract, salt and spices. Mix together well. Take 1/3 of this pumpkin pie mixture and add to the butter chocolate mixture and mix well. Repeat until all pumpkin mixture is incorporated into the chocolate mixture.

Pour batter into prepared chocolate pie crust and bake in oven at 350 degrees for one hour. Transfer pie to wire rack to cool.

To serve, melt 1 ½ ounces of milk chocolate on top of pie. Serve with whipped cream if desired.

Banana Pumpkin Mousse Pie

This pie is like the classic pumpkin mousse full of flavor. It just happens to be a pumpkin banana pie.

Ingredients

Crust
2 ½ cups of finely crushed graham cracker crumbs
½ cup of sugar
½ teaspoon of cinnamon
½ cup of butter, melted

Filling
½ cup of half and half
15 ounces of canned pumpkin

1 cup of brown sugar
1 teaspoon of salt
1 teaspoon of cinnamon
½ teaspoon of nutmeg
3 egg yolks
2 teaspoons of gelatin, unflavored
1 mashed ripe banana
1 teaspoon of grated orange zest
½ cup of heavy cream
2 tablespoons of sugar

Topping:
1 cup of heavy cream

¼ cup of sugar
½ teaspoon of vanilla
Orange zest

Directions

Preheat oven to 350F.

Into a bowl, combine sugar, cinnamon, the finely crushed graham cracker crumbs and the melted butter and mix together well. Press evenly into the bottom and up the sides of an 11-inch tart pan. Bake for about 10 – 12 min and then cool.

Make the filling: Into a heat-proof bowl submerged into a simmering a hot water bath, heat the pumpkin, hal and half, salt, brown sugar, nutmeg and sugar for about 5 min.

Meanwhile, into another bowl, whip the egg yolks, mix in portion of the hot pumpkin, stir then pour back into the heated bowl of pumpkin mixture. Heat and stir the mixture over the simmering water for another 4 to 5 min or until starts to thicken. Take the mixture off of heat.

Into a bowl, dissolve the gelatin into ¼ cup of cold water; and mix into pumpkin mixture. Add the orange zest and the mashed banana, mix well. Set aside and allow to cool.

Into another mixing bowl, whisk the heavy cream until soft peaks form.

Whisk in the sugar until firm peaks form. Fold th whipped cream into the pumpkin mixture and spread into the cooled tart shell. Refrigerate for 2 hrs. to overnight to set

Make the topping: Into a mixing bowl, whip the heavy cream until soft peaks form. Add the sugar and vanilla and whisk until firm peaks form. Pipe decoratively on the pie and sprinkle orange zest. Serve chilled.

Maple-Walnut Pumpkin Pie

The maple and pumpkin filling comes so blended with the crunchy walnut streusels and topping.

Ingredients

Crust, 9-inch:
1 cup of all-purpose flour
1/2 teaspoon of salt
1/4 cup of canola oil
3 tablespoon of cold water

Filling:
1 (15oz) can of pumpkin
1 (14 oz.) can of sweetened condensed milk
2 whole eggs
2 tablespoon real maple syrup
1 1/2 teaspoon of pumpkin pie spice

Streusel:
2 tablespoon of all-purpose flour

1/4 cup of packed brown sugar
1/4 cup of walnuts, finely chopped
2 tablespoon of cold butter

Topping:
1 cup of whipping cream

2 tablespoon of packed brown sugar
chopped walnuts, if desired

Direction

Prepare pie crust. Into a bowl combine flour with salt, mix well. Mix oil and water and pour into the flour mixture, mix until well incorporated. Add more flour or water until desired dough is attained. Roll over in between two wax paper sheets forming a disk and chill for about 30 min. Preheat oven to 425F.

Into a bowl, combine all filling ingredients, beat to blend. Spread into crust-lined pan and bake for about 10 min.

Meanwhile, into a small bowl, mix flour, sugar, and walnuts; cut in butter until crumbly. Set streusel aside.

Reduce oven heat to 350F. Sprinkle streusel over pie. Loosely cover crust edge with foil to avoid over- browning. Bake about 33 min longer or until toothpick inserted comes out clean. Cool completely.

Prepare topping. Into a bowl, whisk whipping cream and brown sugar until soft crests form. Serve pie with whipped cream and garnish with chopped walnuts.

Persimmon-Pumpkin Pie

This easy and quick recipe produces a buttery pumpkin pie and with a little tangy twist.

Ingredients:

- 1 – 8 inch pie crust, unbaked
- 1 cup of canned pumpkin puree
- 1 cup of persimmon pulp

- ½ cup of cream cheese
- ½ cup of sugar

- ½ cup of heavy whipping cream
- 1 tablespoon of cornstarch
- ¼ teaspoon of salt
- 1 ½ teaspoons of pumpkin pie spice
- 4 eggs

Directions

Preheat the oven to 350F. Fit the unbaked pie shell into 8-inch pie pan.

Combine the persimmon and the pumpkin into a food processor and then blend the ingredients together until they are smooth. Add cream cheese, sugar, cornstarch, salt, pumpkin pie spice, the eggs and the whipping cream and blend until all are well incorporated. Spread the pie filling into the pie prepared crust and bake for 45 - 50 min or until it the pie is firm and a toothpick inserted into or near the center comes away clean.

Serve with whipped cream.

Toffee Pumpkin Pie

Ingredients:

1 prepared pie crust
15 ounces of pumpkin puree
1 cup of sugar
1 tablespoon of flour
2 teaspoons of cinnamon
2 eggs, beaten
1 ½ teaspoons of vanilla
1 cup of half and half
1 cup of toffee chips

Directions:

Preheat oven to 375 degrees.

Stir together sugar, flour, pumpkin and cinnamon in a large mixing bowl until well combined. Add the vanilla and eggs and beat together lightly. Stir in the half and half.

Pour pie filling into prepared pie crust. Sprinkle toffee chips on top.

Bake pie in preheated oven for 40 – 45 minutes until a toothpick inserted in the center of the pie comes out clean.

Transfer to a wire baking rack to cool for an hour and then cover pie and chill in fridge or at least 4 hours.

Chocolate Cream Pumpkin Pie

Ingredients

3 whole eggs

1/4 cup of light brown sugar, packed

1/8 teaspoon of ground cinnamon

1/8 teaspoon of ground nutmeg

1/2 teaspoon of vanilla extract

2 cups of heavy cream, divided

1 (15-ounce) can of pumpkin puree

2 (9-ounce) packages of chocolate wafer cookies

16 ounces of mascarpone cheese

1 tablespoon of sugar

1/2 cup pumpkin seeds, no shells, roughly chopped, toasted

Directions

Into a large mixing bowl whisk eggs, sugar, cinnamon, nutmeg and vanilla until smooth.

Into a saucepan, bring to simmer 1 cup of cream and the pumpkin puree over low heat with stirring. Pour about a cup of the hot pumpkin mixture into the egg mixture and whisk until blended. Pour back into the pumpkin mixture, stir and simmer for another minute. Put off heat and set aside to cool.

Layer chocolate wafers into the bottom of a 9-inch spring form cake pan. Fill gaps with broken pieces.

Add in mascarpone into the cooled pumpkin cream whisk to combine. Spread evenly about 1 cup of pumpkin cream over the cookie layer. Put another cookie layer over the cream and more cream over the cookies. Repeat the layering until all the cookies and cream are used up and ending up with a cookie layer.

Whip the remaining 1 cup heavy cream with 1 tablespoon sugar until stiff crests form. Spread the cream over the pie. Cover with plastic wrap and chill for at least 4 hrs. to overnight.

Remove pie from the cake pan, sprinkle the top with toasted pumpkin seeds and serve.

Pumpkin Banana Mousse Pie

Ingredients

1 premade deep dish pie crust

FILLING:

½ cup of half and half

15 ounces of canned pumpkin

1 cup of brown sugar

1 teaspoon of salt

1 teaspoon of cinnamon

½ teaspoon of nutmeg

3 egg yolks

2 teaspoons of gelatine, unflavored

1 mashed, ripe banana

1 ½ teaspoons of grated orange zest

½ cup of heavy whipping cream

3 tablespoons of white sugar

TOPPING:

1 cup of heavy whipping cream

½ cup of sugar

1 teaspoon of vanilla

Extra orange zest for the topping

Directions:

Preheat the oven to 350F.

Prepare the filling. Set a heat-proof bowl over a bath of simmering hot water. Combine into the bowl, half and half, pumpkin, sugar, salt and spices. Whisk for 5 min until mixture becomes hot.

Meanwhile, in a separate mixing bowl, whisk together the egg yolks. Gradually stir in about ½ cup of the hot pumpkin mixture into the egg yolks until the egg mixture becomes warmed as well. Pour this mixture back into the heated cream, mixing well. Heat and stir further the mixture for another 4 to 5 min, until starts to thicken. Pull the warm pumpkin mixture from the heat.

Into a bowl, dissolve gelatine in ¼ cup of cold water. Pour into pumpkin mixture, together with orange zest and banana and then mix well. Set aside to cool.

Into another bowl, whisk heavy cream until soft crests form. Add sugar and continue whisking until firm crests form. Fold into the pumpkin mixture and pour everything into the deep dish pie crust. Chill it for at least 4 hours.

Prepare the topping. Into a bowl, whip heavy cream until soft crests form. Add sugar and vanilla and continue whisking until firm crests form. Pipe it decoratively on the pie and sprinkle with orange zest. Serve chilled

Vanilla Pumpkin Pie

This is a more mild pumpkin pie.

Ingredients

- 3 cups of canned pumpkin
- 12 ounces of evaporated milk
- 2 eggs
- 1 cup of sugar
- 1 tablespoon of flour
- ¼ teaspoon of salt
- 2 teaspoons of vanilla
- ½ teaspoon of pumpkin pie spice
- 1 premade pie shell, 9 inches

Direction

Preheat oven to 450F.

Into a large mixing bowl, combine all ingredients, mix to blend. Spread filling into prepared pastry shell and bake for about 20 min. Decrease oven heat to 350F and bake further for another 40 min until it passes the toothpick doneness test.

Cool completely on a wire rack before serving.

Pumpkin Walnut Pie

Ingredients:

Crust

- 3 cups of walnuts
- 1 teaspoon of baking soda
- ½ teaspoon of salt
- 3 tablespoons of butter, melted

Filling

- 15 ounces of canned pumpkin
- 1 cup of coconut milk
- 1 ½ teaspoons of vanilla
- ½ teaspoon of ground cloves
- 1 teaspoon of cinnamon
- 1 teaspoon of nutmeg
- ½ teaspoon of ginger
- ½ teaspoon of cardamom
- ¼ teaspoon of salt
- 3 tablespoons of maple syrup

3 eggs, beaten

Direction

Preheat oven to 350F.

Into a food processor, blend walnuts, baking soda and salt until finely ground. Add butter and pulse blended.

Scrape and spread batter into the bottom and up the sides of a 9-inch pie pan. Place pan on a cookie sheet and bake for about 15 min. Cool on wire rack.

Prepare the filling. Into a bowl, mix all ingredients, spread into the pre-baked crust and bake for 50 min. or until the centre is firm and inside jiggle. Cool completely before cutting into wedges. Serve with a dollop of whipped cream.

Caramel-Pecan Pumpkin Pie

It is delicious! The caramelized topping adds real depth to this classic pumpkin flavour.

Ingredients

1/4 teaspoon of ground nutmeg

1 (15 oz.) can of pumpkin puree

1/8 teaspoon of ground allspice

1/4 cup of shortening, melted

1/4 cup of light cream

1/4 teaspoon of salt

1/4 teaspoon of ground cinnamon

1/2 cup of brown sugar

4-5 tablespoons of cold water

1 tablespoon of all-purpose flour

2 tablespoons of butter, melted

1/2 cup of pecans

1 teaspoon of lemon peel

1/2 cup of granulated sugar

- 1/2 teaspoon of vanilla

- 1/4 teaspoon of salt

- 2 whole eggs

- 1 1/4 cups of all-purpose flour

Direction

Preheat oven to 375F.

Into a mixing bowl combine flour and salt, mix well. Cut in shortening until crumbly. Gradually add water, a tbsp. at a time, mixing after every addition until firm dough is formed. Form dough into a ball.

On a floured surface; roll out the dough to form a 12-inch disk. Pat and fit into sides and bottom of a 9-inch pie pan. Trim edges to leave ½-inch overhang; fold under and flute edges. Set aside.

Into a large bowl, mix pumpkin puree, eggs and half and half. Stir in flour, sugar, lemon peel, salt, vanilla and spices until fully blended. Spread pumpkin pie filling into the pie crust. Loosely cover edges with foil and bake for about 25 min.

In another mixing bowl, mix together the pecans, brown sugar and the butter until well combined. Remove foil from the pie and then drizzle the brown sugar mixture on the pie. Bake for another 20 min more or until a toothpick inserted comes out clean and topping is golden and filling is bubbly.

Cool on a wire rack. Cover and chill for 2 hrs. before serving.

Spicy Pumpkin Pie

Ingredients

2 tablespoons of all-purpose flour

1/2 teaspoon of salt

2/3 cup of packed brown sugar

1/2 cup of white sugar

1/8 teaspoon of ground cloves

1/8 teaspoon of ground ginger

1/2 teaspoon of ground cinnamon

1/8 teaspoon of ground allspice

1 1/2 cups of canned pumpkin puree

2 tablespoons of light molasses, mild-flavoured

3 whole eggs

1 cup of whipping cream

1 frozen pie crust, 9-inch, unbaked

¼ cup walnuts, toasted, chopped

Direction

Place baking sheet in oven and preheat to 450F.

Into a bowl, combine the first eight ingredients, mix to blend. Add in pumpkin, molasses and eggs, whisk to blend. Stir in cream. Spread mixture into prepared pie shell.

Place pie on preheated baking sheet and bake for about 10 min. Decrease oven temperature to 325F and bake further for about 40 min or until sides puff and centre is just set. Cool on wire rack.

Drizzle chopped toasted walnuts around the edge of the pie before serving.

Honey Pumpkin Pie

A great pumpkin pie is a blend of a crisp flaky crust and smooth creamy custard. This is what Honey Pumpkin pie is all about.

Ingredients

1 premade pie shell

Filling:

2 whole eggs

15 ounces of pumpkin puree

1 cup of honey

½ cup of light cream

1 ½ teaspoon of cinnamon

1 teaspoon of cloves

1 teaspoon of ginger

1 teaspoon of nutmeg

1 teaspoon of salt

2 tablespoon of sour cream

2 teaspoons of milk

Direction

Preheat oven to 350F.

Make the pie filling. Into a large mixing bowl, beat the eggs lightly. Mix in the honey, pumpkin puree, light cream, salt and spices and then spread pie filling into pastry shell.

Into another mixing bowl, combine the milk and the sour cream; pipe in spiral pattern all over the filling. Using a fork, make a swirling pattern across the pastry and bake for an hour or until a toothpick comes out clean when inserted. Cool on wire rack.

Pumpkin Mincemeat Pie

The classic pumpkin mincemeat pie blends the aroma of pumpkin and the flavour of mincemeat.

Ingredients

- 1 – 9 inch prepared pie pan
- 1 cup of sugar
- 2 teaspoons of cinnamon
- 1 teaspoon of nutmeg
- ¼ teaspoon of cloves
- 3 beaten eggs
- 2 cups of canned pumpkin puree
- 2 cups of evaporated milk
- 1 cup of mincemeat

Directions:

Preheat oven to 425F.

Into a bowl, combine spices and sugar, mix until blended. Beat in canned pumpkin and eggs. Stir in evaporated milk and set aside.

Spread mincemeat evenly into the pie shell and then evenly spread pumpkin mixture all over the mincemeat.

Place the pie on a baking sheet and bake for about 15 min. Reduce heat to 350F and bake further for 30 – 40 min or until toothpick inserted comes out clean.

Serve warm with whipped cream.

Made in the USA
Las Vegas, NV
02 October 2024